THE INNER CHURCH

OF THE

21 ST

CENTURY

Patrick Isaac

THE INNOVATIVE CHURCH OF THE 21ST CENTURY

Unless otherwise indicated, scriptural quotations are from
the New King James Version of the Bible (NKJV).

iUniverse books may be ordered through booksellers or by contacting:

iUniverse
1663 Liberty Drive
Bloomington, IN 47403
www.iuniverse.com
1-800-Authors (1-800-288-4677)

ISBN: 978-1-4917-4001-9 (sc)
ISBN: 978-1-4917-4002-6 (e)

Printed in the United States of America.

iUniverse rev. date: 10/16/2014

Table of Contents

1   The Innovative Church of the 21st Century   1

2   Technological Turn   4

3   Excellence   9

4   Excellence in Ministers   16

5   Excellence by Perfecting   23

6   Perfecting for the Work of the Ministry   26

7   An Educated Church   33

8   Infiltrating the Political and Governmental Arenas   38

9   Daniel the Prime Minister Prophet   41

10 Joseph the Governor Prophet   46

11 Infiltrating the Marketplace   50

    Teaching the Principles of the Kingdom on Finances   61

    Application of Kingdom Principles of Finances   62

    Penetrate, Affect and Influence the Marketplace   63

    Laying the Finances at the Apostles' Feet for Unfolding the Vision of God   64

1

The Innovative Church
of the 21ˢᵗ Century

M aking the first steps in this new millennium, the Church of Jesus Christ is facing new challenges. It will need to negotiate and overcome these new challenges in order to advance the kingdom of God on earth. Our society, our technology and even our communications and informational systems have changed and are quite different from those of yesterday. Therefore, we cannot hope to conspicuously affect our present society with the methods and ways of yesterday's society. It is imperative for the Church to innovate. I am therefore convinced that only an optimized, innovative, apostolic Church will be capable of making the difference in our present society and "kingdomize" the earth. I define "kingdomizing" as the action of the Church of Jesus Christ advancing and establishing the kingdom of God on earth.

This innovative Church is one that has revelation of its identity and understands that it is not called to sit-in in the four walls of a building, but is sent out to transform its generation for Christ. This Church is not one that comes religiously in a building twice a week to calm its Christian conscience, but rather chosen people who walk toward the fulfillment of their destiny. It is a chosen generation that does not have a form of godliness denying the power thereof, but an educated generation that fully understands the profound revelation of Jesus Christ and the mandate assigned by him. In this generation, God is raising apostles and prophets capable of optimizing the Church for its apostolic mandate. He is raising a new generation of Christians who are not hiding behind their Bible and their eternal life, but are clearly affecting their communities for Christ. It is a new generation which will not be intimidated by what the world will throw at them and say about them, but will be able to show forth the power and authority that Jesus Christ gave them to influence and change the world with the good news of the Gospel of the kingdom. It is a new generation for whom every place their feet shall thread upon will be theirs. This is the Church which will "kingdomize" the earth in this 21st century.

Thus, the apostolic Church which is sent out by the Lord to affect its society will have certain particularities non-negotiable for the success of its destiny. Needless to say, spirituality, holiness, biblical depth and demonstration of the power of Jesus Christ are mandatory to affect the world with the Gospel of the kingdom. Nevertheless, there are certain other elements that I find neglected in the Body of Christ, which the apostolic Church cannot afford to overlook and take lightly. It will need to be innovative, mastering these elements and optimize their application to accentuate the efficacy and efficiency of the propagation of the Gospel in order to kingdomize our territory for Jesus Christ.

2

Technological Turn

In this era, in order to remarkably affect our generation, we will need to maximize the use of our modern-day technology. The Church has had difficulty to follow the technological and communications innovations of its generation. We are in an era where the secular world is on the cutting edge of technology, but the Church is trailing tediously. While a company that respects itself and really wants to have the upper hand in its market equips itself communication-wise, with regards to multimedia and all technological aspects, many ministries do not even have a website. Many of those who do have a website, their websites are in a primitive state. We want to affect and impact the 21st century with a technology, a system, a style, and a message and ministry of the 20th century. The Church of Jesus Christ will need to upgrade in order to allow the Christ who abides in it to be propelled forward with present-day technological advances in order to be fully able to accomplish its mandate in this generation. The technological turn is not negotiable.

The Word of God tells us in Proverbs 11.30 that he who wins souls is wise. It will take wisdom to win souls for the Lord in this 21st century. In fact, in any given era, the ministers who mark their times and seasons by the excellence of their accomplishment of the Great Commission certainly use God-given wisdom.

As we take a look at the strategies and tools used by the Lord Jesus to affect his generation with the Gospel, we can clearly see the use of divine wisdom. He capitalized on the tools available to him in his time to maximize the propagation of the Gospel. Although he did not have cordless microphones, the Lord used the waves of the waters to help his voice travel. Since fishing was an economic strength in his time and crowds would clutter by the sea shore, he would speak to numerous people from a little boat on the sea shores of Galilee to proclaim the message of the kingdom. The Lord, to avoid the difficulty of being poorly understood by the thousands of people who came to listen in his conferences, talked to the multitude from the top of a hill or a mountain to allow his voice to travel better, and thus be heard more clearly.

We also see in Jerusalem, on the last day, the great day of the feast, he stood out before the crowd and cried out: "If anyone is thirsty, let him come and drink..." In order to attract the attention of the majority, he used this necessary technique in his time, not having other resources to announce his message. Jesus capitalized on the numerous people in the city who came and gathered for the *Feast of Tabernacles*. This technique was quite successful since he brought the crowd to think and even brought some to realize that *he* was the Christ of God. Unfortunately, some Christians of our era, who refuse to evolve, still use this kind of technique to try to spread the Good News of Jesus Christ in large metropolitan cities. Is it successful? It is, more or less, since it brings a number of conversions. But very often this technique of evangelism leads more to confusion than anything else, because these followers are very often religious Christians who have little training and who are not at all called to pursue this type of ministry.

I still remember as an adolescent being harassed by those religious people who were evangelizing at the doors of the metro stations shouting: "Choose Jesus or go to hell!!!" I wonder if they took the time to read The Great Commission of our Lord Jesus who commands us to go preach a good and not a bad news. I do not believe it is wise to make such a crude parallel between salvation and hell.

We would be really naïve to think that the Lord, filled with divine wisdom, would not have maximized our modern day technology to proclaim the Gospel of the kingdom with other tools much more productive than shouting in the middle of a crowded intersection on a day of festivities. Yet, many who consider themselves being filled with the Holy Spirit work with a limited or even outdated technology, relying simply on the Word and the power of the Holy Spirit, but forgetting that God gave them an intelligence too, which they can appeal to and use when called to preach the Gospel. Many servants of God who have a great anointing and a powerful word of the Lord will be disqualified in this season if they do not make the technological turn. We may be spiritual, but the Internet and all the technology surrounding it is essential in this generation for anyone who wants to make an "impact" and dominate his field. Surely, the ministry of the Gospel is not exempted. The ministers and the array of ministries in our era will have to find ways to maximize the World Wide Web to proclaim the Gospel effectively.

What a blessing to have, in our era, communications systems able to broadcast a man in a given geographical area to a multitude of other places simultaneously. So without even moving, several people miles away can be transformed by the Gospel of Jesus Christ without being physically present where the preaching takes place and being in the presence of the messenger who spreads out God's Word.

Imagine the potential for evangelism which exists with the method of forwarding email addresses. By this manner, if a person has been blessed by a message which he has listened to on a particular web site that offers the option to forward the message to ten friends, the multiplication method can potentially reach thousands of people in a matter of some forwarded emails per person. Many companies have already made their fortunes and acquired renown in their domain by the ingenuity of the *Net* notwithstanding television and radio which have an increasingly larger pool of listeners. When will the Church awaken from technological mediocrity and decisively take the world with the Gospel of the kingdom? We are a mile ahead having on our side the God who created heaven and earth in whom resides all authority; it is more than time to fully benefit from this fact.

The Bible says in Romans 10.14,
"How shall they believe in Him of whom they have not heard?..."

There are manifold ways of communications so that this generation can hear of Jesus; it is the responsibility of the Church to quicken its feet to enter full force in the world of communication and master it to accomplish its mandate, in this era. Certainly, a technological shift is necessary in this informed and computerized generation.

3

Excellence

I can still remember the negative image I had of the Church in the years that preceded my new birth. The congregations which I had the opportunity to visit were bluntly mediocre. The people of God that I saw had the apparels of the early eighties, late seventies although we were in the early nineties. Their hairstyles, their clothes, and their shoes were totally strange to me. Their sound systems were in intensive care with life support preparing to leave a coma and give up the ghost. Some could say, as they are reading this, that the flesh is worthless, it is the Spirit who gives life, the spiritual man is dead to the things of this world. They may go on uttering or thinking of verses which they only beleaguer by using them out of context. Know that the first "impact" we have as the Sent Ones of God is our external "impact". The common mortal who does not know yet your spirituality will associate what he sees from your natural to your God.

> The Bible declares, talking about King Saul in 1 Samuel 9.2, *"And he had a choice and handsome son whose name was Saul. There was not a more handsome person than he among the children of Israel. From his shoulders upward he was taller than any of the people."*

1 Samuel 16.12, talking about King David, says,
"...Now he was ruddy, with bright eyes, and good-looking..."

These verses explicitly present a quality that is necessary for a servant of God. Notice that in the choice of King Saul, as well as the choice of King David, the Lord took the time to mention the excellence of their appearances. He chose young men who were well-presented. They were good-looking. Is it not therefore relevant to think that an impeccable appearance raises the credibility of a King? What can we consequently say of a King who looks more like a slave than a prince? Would this give any glory to the King of kings?

The Lord took a whole chapter, Exodus 28, to describe the beauty necessary for the garments of the priests. How can our Lord want and expect excellence for the priests in the Old Testament and mediocrity for his kingdom of priests, his saints who are heirs of God and joint-heirs with Christ according to Romans 8.17? Henceforth when a Christian dons mediocrity, the image he is projecting to the non-believer is that he is serving a mediocre God, a God who takes pleasure in the suffering and mediocrity of his servants. What a terrible lie about the God of Abraham, Isaac and Jacob who takes pleasure in the prosperity of His servants, Psalms 35.27. The God of gods, the Lord God is excellent. He desires therefore that his children be excellent and have excellence.

What a contrast between the temple and the ministers of the Old Testament and the mediocrity which we find in many churches and modern ministers! I am not the advocate of ministers who abuse and waste the finances of the kingdom, but it is imperative for us to realize that if we want the Church to be an oasis where everyone can come to drink the word of life, it needs to be in a position to welcome the average man and woman, the beggar, as well as the rich man, the general worker, as well as the professional. The time has come for the Church to be impeccable in its presentation. I have quite a hard time to believe that the Lord Jesus living in the 21st century would function in mediocrity to make disciples of the nations. I really do not believe he would use a small boat to cross the Atlantic to bring the Gospel to America. I truly believe though that the Lord would have used the necessary means to affect the world with the Gospel. Most assuredly, he would have capitalized on the cutting-edge technology and advanced communications systems of our era to release salvation through the World Wide Web and airwaves.

For a long time, many ignorant Christians had supported a Gospel of mediocrity believing that piety was synonymous to mediocrity. The great tragedy in this lie of the devil is that many leaders taught this heresy. It is therefore not surprising to see a multitude of religious and ignorant Christians drown in poverty, for they believe and make vows of piety which is an evident token of this theological lunacy. But the devil is a liar, this time is over! The innovative Church of the 21st century is rising up and bringing a wind of resurrection, raising the Body of Christ from heresies and the ignorance taught for many years and taking it out of its rickety and poor state following the mediocrity of its revelation. Through apostolic and prophetic preaching and teaching, the Body of Christ will be able to grasp the will of God who desires to give us what is best for us. Thereby we will be able to bring forth an excellent ministry to the level of the excellent God we serve. Know that the Church is called to be on the cutting-edge of technology to maximize its capacity to proclaim the Gospel of Jesus Christ. As long as the instruments used remain a means and not the ultimate goal. We should be seeking God and doing his perfect will and not seeking sumptuous material goods. The Word exhorts us, not to love the world and the things of the world. However this truth does not exempt us from using the things of the world to maximize the preaching of the Gospel.

How unfortunate it is when discussions amongst believers, or even amongst leaders, turn around the fact of having a multidimensional multimillion dollar building instead of discussing things pertinent to the advancement of the kingdom! Men of God, let us be strategic and faithful stewards of the finances of God who owns the world and the riches thereof, by using all the modern means possible with wisdom to tremendously affect and impact our society. Let us do this with our eyes focused on Jesus, the author and finisher of our faith without letting ourselves be hoodwinked and seduced by the things of this world.

Many local churches need an upgrade, and this upgrade needs to take place quickly. Or else do not be surprised that the only ones they will be able to attract to come and sit on their church pews are those stricken and without hope of getting above the threshold of poverty and mediocrity. For it would be quite difficult to solicit and attract a professional with a good standard of living to come and sit on church pews with chicken bone leftovers and chewing gum in a badly ventilated room without an air conditioning system in a metropolitan city with humid and torrid summers, with bathrooms having toilets, which have difficulty completing their flushing cycles. The Church absolutely needs to manifest excellence in its strategic position in this era where excellence is a criterion for success.

The Bible says in Isaiah 2.1-3,
"The word that Isaiah the son of Amoz saw concerning Judah and Jerusalem; Now it shall come to pass in the latter days that the mountain of the Lord's house shall be established on the top of the mountains, and shall be exalted above the hills; and all nations shall flow to it. Many people shall come and say, 'Come, and let us go up to the mountain of the Lord, to the house of the God of Jacob; he will teach us His ways, and we shall walk in His paths.' For out of Zion shall go forth the law and the word of the Lord from Jerusalem."

I believe this word of the Lord given to Prophet Isaiah concerns not only the Church of the first century, but also has relevance for the innovative Church that will advance the kingdom of God in this era.

That word tells us that the house of the Lord will be established on top of the mountains. The apostolic Church will be raised up and exalted amidst the nations of the earth. It will be exalted to dominate, exalted to make an impact, and exalted to multiply itself. The innovative apostolic Church is exalted to be exposed. We also need to know that there is another side to elevation and exaltation. You see exaltation will impose demonstration, exaltation demands confirmation. Therefore the Lord tells us that many nations shall come and say: "Come and let us go up to the mountain of the Lord, to the house of the God of Jacob..." Truly, it is the mission of the Church of Jesus Christ to attract the nations. Many leaders of Churches most certainly dream of the accomplishment of this prophecy in their Church and ministry, wanting that the multitudes flow into their services.

Nevertheless, it is necessary to know that the multitudes which will flow into the assemblies will have expectancy as they fill up the house of the Lord. Even though the non-believers can be backbiters and condescending toward the Church, the great majority of them have a set image of the way the Church should look. In their views of the Lord's house, they see cleanliness, solemnity, respect, and excellence. What a surprise it would be for them if they would enter a church and see dirtiness, disorder, a lack of respect for the ministers of God, for the service and of the house of God. Unfortunately, this occurrence is too common in the Body of Christ. People of God, the time has come for us to flow in a higher dimension of excellence. The Church is called to raise its bar of excellence.

The Christians can no longer hide their mediocrity behind religious Christian sayings. These sayings tend to reveal one's ignorance of the Word, as well as laziness in striving for excellence which emanates from the Gospel, rather than spirituality in the Word of God. The Church will no longer be able to bypass excellence if it wants to affect the different sectors of our modern society.

4

Excellence in Ministers

1 Peter 4.10-11 declares,

> *"As each one has received a gift, minister it to one another, as good stewards of the manifold grace of God. If anyone speaks, let him speak as the oracles of God. If anyone ministers, let him do it as with the ability which God supplies, that in all things God may be glorified through Jesus Christ, to whom belong the glory and the dominion forever and ever. Amen."*

Our Lord calls the Church to be excellent. For it to function in a high level of excellence, its ministers need to function in excellence in their respective ministries and anointing. Every minister needs therefore to put at the service of the Body of Christ the gifts he has received from the Lord. Apostle Peter inspired by the Holy Spirit declares, "... if anyone ministers; let him do it as with the ability which God supplies." People of God, the ministry that you bring in the work of God, do it according to the ability that you received from God. Do not be an usher if you have not received that grace; do not seek to be a soloist or a musician if you have not received from God that grace.

1 CORINTHIANS 12.29-30
"Are all apostles? Are all prophets? Are all teachers? Are all workers of miracles? Do all have gifts of healings? Do all speak with tongues? Do all interpret?"

All cannot be apostles; all cannot be prophets. All cannot be David; the Body of Christ also needs some Joabs.

Joab, the chief of David's army, understood this preponderant principle of excellence in the ministry of God and because of that, he fulfilled well his ministry.

The Bible says in 2 Samuel 12.26-29,
"Now Joab fought against Rabbah of the people of Ammon, and took the royal city. And Joab sent messengers to David, and said, 'I have fought against Rabbah, and I have taken the city's water supply. Now therefore, gather the rest of the people together and encamp against the city and take it, lest I take the city and it be called after my name.' So David gathered all the people together and went to Rabbah, fought against it, and took it."

We see in this episode of the Scriptures, Joab the captain of the army of David with his troop refusing to penetrate into the city of Rabbah after having conquered it, for he acknowledged that this glory pertains to the king. What an impressive sign of humility and of revelation of ministry. I am sure that many carnal ministers would have invaded and would have taken, with pleasure, that city and even start their own kingdom, having the insatiable thirst for power and glory. But Joab had the revelation of his position. He was blessed with his role and he was excellent in it. You might not be an apostle, but a great prophet. You might not be a prophet, but an usher with a special anointing for business. What an anointing breaker, to have ministers ministering without grace! So many services are without messages because of improvised preachers! Or consider the number of praise and worship sessions that bothers more than anything else because the singers and musicians *almost* have the right key.

If someone ministers let him minister according to the ability that God communicates. In the search for excellence in ministry, it is important to know that all ministers have the potential for excellence when they are in their God-given position. For God who divinely assigns also gives the capacity and gift to accomplish the assignment. The faster the Church relinquishes the spirit of competition, jealousy and envy, the faster the members of the Body of Christ will be able to be efficient in their respective positions.

The Bible says in Ephesians 4.16,
"From whom the whole body, joined and knit together by what every joint supplies, according to the effective working by which every part does its share, causes growth of the body for the edifying of itself in love."

The Word gives us revelation on the importance of positioning for every part in the Body of Christ for its growth. Kingdom growth is drawn from the effective working by which every part does its share in its strength and proper positioning. Every member of the Body of Christ has its strength and its own capacity. It is imperative to know that in order for a minister to even aspire to be excellent and minister in excellence, he primarily has to be in his God-given position with his God-given capacity. There is a polemic that definitely needs to be resolved in the Body of Christ: the importance for the saints to be in their positions.

Prophet Habakkuk declared in Habakkuk 2.1-2,
"I will stand my watch and set myself on the rampart, and watch to see what He will say to me, and what I will answer when I am corrected."

It is interesting to read that Prophet Habakkuk declared that he stood at his watch. In other words he was in his rank, in his position. Prophet Habakkuk was neither in the position of Prophet Jeremiah, nor the position of King David, but was in his position. Know that each saint who is part of the Body of Christ has a position pre-destined to him before the foundation of the world. Therefore we should not be searching for which position to choose, but rather the position which God pre-destined for us. This revelation, when fully grasped, will eliminate a lot of carnality in the Church, because numerous battles of the flesh would stop. Envy, jealousy and competition among other fleshly things would have more difficulty to show their faces in the normal life of the Church. Often, a minister desiring to minister with quality to his God in his respective position, has more opposition from the carnal brothers in the Church than from the non-believers. One would be surprised to know how many ministerial oppression comes from a carnal brother's or sister's envy or jealousy who refuses to concentrate on his prophetic role in the army of God, but wastes his time nurturing jealousy and envy of someone else's grace.

Yet, the Word tells us that it is not he who commends himself who is approved, but he who God commends. Therefore, even if you are frustrated by the prophetic apostolic grace of a brother or sister, or the special anointing of praise and worship that a minister releases in ministry, you will never be able to flow in the same level if God has not granted you the necessary gifting, nor mandated you to minister in the same position and ministry.

The Bible says in Proverbs 14.30,
"... Envy is rottenness to the bones."

Bone cancer is an extremely painful sickness, which destroys internally. Everyone perceives your pain, but cannot physically see it. They can only see your intense pain by your bodily expressions and words. Envy is such a cancer that grinds and destroys internally.

Many would not see it, but it is a painful spiritual disease that destroys internally the carnal Christian. The more spiritual ones can see it if the Lord gives them discernment, but the carnal Christian suffers painfully and bitterly.

Therefore do not let envy destroy you piece by piece. Realize that God is the author and the giver of the gifts and the positions in his Body. When someone is in his position, do yourself a favor: glorify God and maximize your energy in recognizing and maximizing your position to do your part in bringing growth in the Body.

Many Christians have a problem hearing the voice of God because they are not in their position. But the Prophet Habakkuk was able to hear what God had to say because he was in his watch. The guidelines that will permit you to accomplish your destiny will be given to you in your watch. It is therefore normal to have spiritual interference in hearing God when you are not in your position designated by God. You will not only have difficulty to receive from God, but you can also be detrimental to the team of God. Imagine yourself on a soccer team, with a goalie who wants to improvise himself as the striker or a defenseman who wants to venture as a winger. The team can have the elite in each position, but if they are not in their position, a team with lesser talent, but with their players in the right position can easily defeat them.

I would like to go deeper in the revelation of the positioning of the ministers in the Body of Christ. Three saints can be governmental prophets and have similar prophetic gifting and miss their calling by being assigned in the wrong positions. We therefore need not only to be called and trained, but also mandated by God in our position if we want to fully succeed in our calling. It is not sufficient to say, "I am called and trained," but are you mandated by God in the ministry that you are doing, in the position that you are in? Prophet Habakkuk was at his watch and not in Prophet Jeremiah's or Prophet Ezekiel's position. Therefore, he was able to receive the word of the Lord. He was not where he wanted to be, but where the Lord wanted him to be. Sometimes, unfortunately, a Christian can be where he wants to be without necessarily being where God wants him to be. My question for you is: Are you in your God-given position?

5

Excellence by Perfecting

EPHESIANS 4.11-12

"And he gave some, apostles; and some, prophets; and some, evangelists; and some, pastors and teachers; for the PERFECTING OF THE SAINTS, for the work of ministry, for the edifying of the body of Christ"[1]

MATTHEW 5.48

"Therefore you shall be PERFECT, just as your Father in heaven is perfect."

It is one thing to be in position, but the Lord requires us to be excellent in our position. The minister who strives to give his best to the Lord should also strive for excellence in the ministry. Therefore, to have excellence in ministry, the ministers need to be in their position maximizing their God-given abilities. This excellence requires the minister to sharpen the expertise of his gifting. Even if a minister has a natural talent, he should still thrive to perfect it. The innate oratory grace of a minister does not exempt him from seeking to improve with personal or academic study of homiletics. Excellence is not a function of the gift but the effort invested in the gift.

---

[1] King James Version (KJV)

As the secular world seeks excellence in what it offers, how can the Church think of affecting this world without offering it excellence? Sometimes it is not the message that the world rejects, but the appearance of the Church bringing it. Let us therefore be people who seek to perfect our excellence. Although the ministry gifts bring spiritual perfecting to the saints of the Body of Christ, it is nevertheless the work of the saints to also seek to perfect their graces and gifts by technical improvement that will enable them to be perfect as the heavenly Father is perfect.

The Lord told Jeremiah in Jeremiah 1.5 that before he was formed in the womb of his mother, He had called him as a prophet to the nations. Although we are born with the gifts that God had prepared for us before the foundation of the world, we still need to perfect them. We cannot work to receive the gifts of God, but we are called to work to perfect them. The soloist therefore has no excuse not to take some singing lessons to better his vocalization. The musician who can play by ear, should not take this as the epitome, but seek to read notes and upgrade his expertise by being able to play with partitions.

Therefore, even though you have a great preaching gift, this does not exempt you from the study of hermeneutics and homiletics to ameliorate your art. Moreover, the study of the Word is a must, given that teachers will receive a stricter judgment. So, in order to avoid story-telling rather than imparting life to the children of God, our preparation as preachers should not stop at the anointing, but information and revelation of the Word need to be added to it. Church of Jesus Christ, let us raise the standard of excellence. It is not enough to be anointed, but anointed and excellent.

6

Perfecting for the Work
of the Ministry

The Bible says in Ephesians 4.11-12,

> *"And he gave some, apostles; and some, prophets; and some,
> evangelists... for the perfecting of the saints, FOR THE WORK OF
> THE MINISTRY..."*[2]

God in his omniscience knew that one man or one ministry
gift would not be able to perfect his people. He therefore
gave five ministerial offices to provide for that task. The pastoral
office is only one of the five-fold ministry gifts necessary for the
perfecting of the saints. It is important to notice that the apostolic
office has primacy. God does not only list it first in verse 11, but also
lists it first in 1 Corinthians 12.28 as he denotes the offices set in the
Church. The apostolic office should not be seen as an honorific title or
a position of the past, but as a leadership office that is in the Church
of Jesus Christ. The apostle should be in spiritual authority in the
Church, regardless of the period of history, knowing the efficiency
of the Word of God. The Lord, a strategist par excellence, who

---

[2] King James Version (KJV)

has instituted the apostolic office in a position of leadership in the Church, had His reasons for that choice. The apostle has the spiritual authority in the Church to give birth to an apostolic people.

With the collaboration and unity of the other five-fold ministers of Ephesians 4.11, the Church is called to be perfected for the work of ministry.

MARK 16.15

"And he said to them, 'Go into all the world and preach the gospel to every creature.'"

MATTHEW 28.19

"Go therefore and make disciples of all the nations..."

The only mandate the Lord gave his disciples is to go preach the Gospel to all nations. The Church of Jesus Christ is an apostolic Church, a Church which is perfected to be sent out. Notice that Mark 16.15 does not tell us to stay, but to go. One of the greatest tragedies of the normal life of the Church is the fact that the saints are oriented towards staying in the house of the Lord instead of going to the world. Many believe they hit the epitome by coming to church two or three times a week, although they just practice a religious ritual. In fact, even those who do attend Church services to receive weekly from the Lord have to understand that this is not enough. The Lord did not say to come, but to go make disciples.

Our service is not rendered complete if it only pertains in coming and receiving in the assemblies of the saints. The apostolic Church fulfills its destiny when the saint who comes to receive revelation and blessing from the gathering of the saints goes and affects his environment with the Gospel of Jesus Christ. This innovative Church understands that the services are periods of refueling to fill one another with the principles and the truths of the kingdom.

Afterwards, they must be sent out into the different fields in their communities to advance the kingdom of God on earth.

It is important to realize that the gathering of the saints is a time for refueling. To bring understanding, we could compare Church assemblies to a gas station. Notice that all normal drivers never come to a gas station to stay. They do not park their car in the filling station, but they fill up and go. The time has come for the ministers of God to adopt that same philosophy. The innovative apostolic Church must understand that the gathering of the saints is a period of filling up with the principles and the truths of the kingdom. People of God, realize that the gathering of the saints is a time of filling up. A place to have spiritual fill up. It is not normal for the saints not to feel the need to go in their own separate ways and fulfill the mandate that God gave to make disciples of all nations.

Nowadays, many believers suffer from spiritual bulimia: an overdose of spiritual information and revelation. This problem is so bad that the devil has injected in some, a spiritual passivity. The interest to be apostolically sent out to win souls has been substituted by carnal Christians seeking for more and more revelational depth. This trend brings absolutely no growth to the Body of Christ and to the kingdom of God, but only the manifestation of saints infested by Leviathan pridefully ministering to one another the word of the Lord. Therefore, instead of using their quality time to share the Gospel to a non-believer, their time is used for futile biblical exchanges with other brethren in the Lord. Nevertheless, the mandate of the Lord is to go... That situation worsens in the fact that many saints have only relationships with Christians, and they do not even put themselves in a position to affect anyone with the Word of God. Nevertheless the mandate is to go...

The Bible says in Mark 3.13-15,

> "And he goeth up into a mountain, and calleth unto Him whom he would: and they came unto him. And he ordained twelve, that they should be with him, and that he might send them forth to preach, and to have power to heal sicknesses, and to cast out devils."[3]

In this portion of the Scriptures the Lord, after taking some time of consecration in prayer on a mountain, chooses the first twelve apostles. He chose twelve so that they may be with him. What was the reason to have the twelve with him? Was our Lord suffering from loneliness or ministerial depression? Absolutely not. But I believe rather, that he wanted the twelve close to him so he could train them. He knew that his ministry was of a short span and that he needed to strategically prepare those who would continue the spreading the Gospel of the kingdom. Therefore, the twelve had quite a privileged training. Being so close to the Master, they had the opportunity to witness the excellence of his character and ministry. They were able to observe closely and learn the fundamentals from the perfect ministerial example. Notice, as we take an eschatological look of the three years of the ministry of our Lord Jesus, the twelve spent more than a year of ministerial observation before being sent out two by two by the Lord to have ministerial practice. The Lord, after identifying them, trained them intensively being constantly with them in his pilgrimage. I truly believe that despite the benefits of Bible institutes and theological seminaries, hands-on training of an apprentice-minister next to an experienced and mature minister is the best kind of training a minister can have. This is so if one truly wants to make an impact for the kingdom of God. Jesus chose the twelve to have them unto him. Now, the ultimate goal of their closeness to the Master was not for them to stay eternally at his side.

---

[3] King James Version (KJV)

The Bible says that after a while, he sent them out two by two and afterwards gave them the Great Commission of making disciples of all nations. Please understand that it is totally unacceptable for saints to spend years at the feet of a servant of God without ever being released in any relevant ministry to bring souls to the Lord. What training and ministerial ignorance! Yet, the Lord optimized three years to prepare his twelve apostles whom afterwards invaded their generation with the Gospel of the kingdom.

Many ministry leaders want to have spiritual sons, but my question is why? Why have many spiritual sons? Is it to make them lose the best years of their lives cheerleading or to train them so they can be sent out?

The ultimate reason why the Lord chose the twelve to be close to him was to send them out to minister. Verse 14 explains this by saying: *"Then He appointed twelve, that they might be with Him and that He might SEND THEM OUT..."* They had the proximity to be trained and to be sent out. It is from this word *send*, in the Greek (*apostoloi*), that come the varying forms of the word apostolic.

Apostle in its smallest common denominator literally means "the sent one." Therefore, the disciples were named apostles because they were sent by the Lord Jesus Christ to fulfill the specific mandate of preaching the good news of the Gospel, heal sicknesses and cast out devils. They had the proximity to go. Henceforth, the purpose of the Lord for his people is not for them to dream to be close to their leaders to make of this a ministry, but to be trained and sent out in the world and make disciples of all nations, heal sicknesses and cast out devils. The twelve were identified, trained and sent out. This is a good summary of an apostolic ministry. An innovative apostolic church is a Church which possesses not only a pastor, but elders of Ephesians 4.11 able to identify and train the saints to then send them in their respective fields to advance the kingdom of God on the earth. The twelve were identified, trained and sent... and you?

A tragedy that is diametrically opposite to the Great Commission of the Lord is the inefficacy of the Church to evangelize the lost world. The Church full of revelation instead of evangelizing proceeds to what I call "exchangelizing."

This is the simple religious act of exchanging saints instead of winning lost souls. The Churches are killing each other over the flock that is already saved in their Churches instead of saving the lost in the nations. The saints that are already saved simply exchange churches and limited or no attention at all is given to the lost that the devil wants to bring to hell. But God is raising an innovative apostolic Church that is trained to go, that is perfected to multiply. This Church is rising up to take its territory, to make an invasion in the nations to translate them from the kingdom of darkness to the kingdom of light.

7

An Educated Church

It is imperative for the Church wanting to "kingdomize" its generation by the Gospel of Jesus Christ, to recognize that it will not be able to fully accomplish its mandate in this 21st century without academic education. Truly, spiritual training is necessary, but academic education still remains preponderant. The need for the saints to optimize their education is not negotiable. As the religious Christians are waiting for the return of the Lord within the four walls of their local church, our society of this 21st century continues its emancipation and growth through education. Society has understood that God has told mankind to subdue and replenish the earth. This passive stand of the Church, while waiting for the return of the Lord, has drowned it in mediocrity in many aspects over the years. The Church has not sought to perfect itself with academic education to be leaders in the secular world. As a consequence the Church is behind in many disciplines in the secular world. The Church needs to educate itself.

There is a saying in the world that states, *knowledge is power.* The Word of God agrees with this saying when it declares in Proverbs 23.23,

> *"Buy the truth, and do not sell it, also wisdom and instruction and understanding."*

For the innovative, apostolic Church to be fully efficient we need to infiltrate, influence and dominate the leadership and the different spheres in our communities. Nevertheless we cannot have penetration in positions of leadership without education. The saints of the Body of Christ need to be educated.

The Bible says in Acts 19.9-10,
"But when some were hardened and did not believe, but spoke evil of the Way before the multitude, he departed from them and withdrew the disciples, reasoning daily in the school of Tyrannus. And this continued for two years so that all who dwelt in Asia heard the word of the Lord Jesus, both Jews and Greeks."

We can see in these verses how the salvation of an educated school director permitted a place for the teaching and preaching of the Gospel by Apostle Paul. He continued there for a span of two years which ultimately affected Asia. The position of leadership of Tyrannus in the sector of education was instrumental in the spreading of the Gospel. Despite the importance of spiritual training, academic training can be a necessary tool to bring credibility and respect as well as increase the decision-making power of ministers of the Gospel in our communities. Do not let the devil and ignorance fool you; people of God, get educated! The Lord shall lead you in your respective disciplines. The more educated you are, the more resources you are able to put in the hands of the Lord to position you in a strategic place of influence to advance the kingdom. Prayer in other tongues will not be able to permit us by itself to take our communities for Jesus. The Body of Christ needs to be strategic. Academic training of its members is one of the prerequisites important for apostolic invasion in our society of this 21st century. Notice that it is much easier to influence a sector where we are ourselves partakers. Although God can use whoever he wants to bring someone to the knowledge of his truth, it is still easier to use a lawyer amidst fellow lawyers in the same firm. On the other hand it might be more complicated for a general Christian worker to witness the Gospel to a professional, because of the difference in social status.

I still remember the day I had to sign our first commercial lease for the building space rented for our church gatherings. One of my elders and I went to see the owner of the building. As we arrived in the office of this businessman, we were directed to his impressive conference room with his accountant, his lawyer, and his realtor who had the responsibility of finding the lessee for his building. Needless to say of the intimidation that the devil wanted to settle in a young minister without any experience in the sector of commercial leasing for buildings. The accountant started speaking to explain certain particularities of the lease. He used some technical terms of business law a course which I took while completing my studies in accounting and business administration in university. He probably thought we were not knowledgeable in the legal terms of commercial leasing and omitted to state some of our rights. I was able to use my knowledge in business law to claim our rights and we were able to consolidate the transaction by God's grace.

The building owner was so impressed that all his intentions were caught by a man he thought was ignorant of business technicalities, and from one who was, to him, only a minister. Now notice, there is nothing dishonorable about being a minister of the Gospel, but his preconceived thoughts were totally shattered. The Lord in his omniscience knows the academic pre-requisite of every minister for every one of his mandates. As we analyze the ministry of Apostle Paul and Peter, we notice that Apostle Paul was the apostle of the gentiles and Apostle Peter was the apostle of the Jews. However we will notice in the study of the Acts of the Apostles the importance the education of Apostle Paul had for the fulfillment of his ministry.

Many times the Lord used his knowledge and his academic background to advance his divine plan. The immensity of the knowledge of Apostle Paul was used greatly to open doors for the propagation of the Gospel of Jesus Christ. He received, because of his academic profile, many opportunities to speak of the Lord in front of dignitaries of his time. Governor Felix and his wife Drusilla in Acts 24.24 listened to Apostle Paul. Festus, the Governor, was so impressed with Apostle Paul's speech that he spoke of him to King Agrippa (in Acts 25.13-14 and 22) who also heard and was conquered by the apologetics of Apostle Paul's faith in Jesus Christ. It would have been virtually impossible for a minister without an educated background to attract that kind of attention and interest from those gentile dignitaries. The Lord certainly knows how to use our academic background for the divine mandate which he has given us.

8

Infiltrating the Political and Governmental Arenas

I strongly believe that there are fields which apostolic people have no choice but to exert an impact on in order to have the advantage in this generation. These sectors will be unavoidable and our God mandates them to be dominated by apostolic ministers. It will be crucial for Christians to infiltrate, influence and strategically dominate these sectors to facilitate the "kingdomizing" of the earth.

For a long time, for many Christians, politics was recognized as a taboo sector. This sector was left to be used by the devil due to carnal and religious leaders of the Church. It is needless to say that the devil, opportunist as he is, took pleasure in controlling this sector of the community recognizing its value in order to permit the advancement of his agenda on earth. But the time has come for the Church to wake up from its slumber and its ignorance, and realize the importance of politics. For the latter, being a sector of authority, dictates the direction a region, a city or any country is taking. Accordingly, this authority, residing in politics, is needed to facilitate the spreading of the Gospel. Therefore, there are Christians who God had predestined before the foundation of the world with the necessary grace and gifts to infiltrate the political arena. They should open their eyes and choose academic areas that will enable them to penetrate this sphere, and thus allow God to open the necessary supernatural doors, so his name will be glorified in the community.

This reluctance in regards to the political arena is incomprehensible when we take into consideration the way God has strategically used statesmen to advance his divine plan on Earth.

9

Daniel the Prime Minister Prophet

DANIEL 1.3-6
"Then the king instructed Ashpenaz, the master of his eunuchs, to bring some of the children of Israel and some of the king's descendants and some of the nobles, young men in whom there was no blemish, but good-looking, gifted in all wisdom, possessing knowledge and quick to understand, who had ability to serve in the king's palace, and whom they might teach the language and literature of the Chaldeans. And the king appointed for them a daily provision of the king's delicacies and of the wine which he drank, and three years of training for them, so that at the end of that time they might serve before the king. Now from among those of the sons of Judah were Daniel, Hananiah, Mishael, and Azariah."

DANIEL 1.17, 20
"As for these four young men, God gave them knowledge and skill in all literature and wisdom.... And in all matters of wisdom and understanding about which the king examined them, he found them ten times better than all the magicians and astrologers who were in all his realm."

In these Scriptures we see the story of Daniel and his companions Hananiah, Mishael and Azariah. The leaders of Babylon saw the potential of these young men and they were sent to school to master the Babylonian culture so they could be used in the service of the king. The Bible says in Daniel 1.17 that God gave them knowledge and skill in all literature and wisdom. These young men were not just graduates from the University of Babylon, but they graduated with honor. The Bible says that they were of an excellent spirit. The king of Babylon was amazed to see that they were ten times superior to the learned who were throughout his kingdom. This should not be surprising since this grace of science, intelligence and wisdom was granted to them by God. The Lord allowed them to be distinguished knowing in his divine plan the way that he would use them to make all recognize the greatness of His name. Not only did the Lord give the necessary grace to the four young Hebrews, he also permitted a situation to elevate them into a position of renown.

It is imperative for us as Christians to know that a man's gift makes room for him, and brings him before great men, Proverbs 18.16. You will not need to make superhuman efforts, manipulate or plot anything for a breakthrough in your propitious sector. But the gifts of a man will make room for him. In Daniel 2.1-18, The Bible says the story of the irritant dreams that King Nebuchadnezzar had and for which he could not find any interpreter. That situation opened a door for Daniel to expose the greatness of his God. History does not mention any carnal effort fomented by Daniel to receive a favor or goodwill from the King.

On the contrary, Daniel 1.9 says,
"Now God had brought Daniel into the favor and goodwill...."

Daniel was under the goodwill of God; the Lord had decided to give him favor. Therefore, the secret of King Nebuchadnezzar's dreams was revealed to Daniel.

He says in the presence of the King in Daniel 2.27-28,

"...The secret which the king has demanded, the wise men, the astrologers, the magicians, and the soothsayers cannot declare to the king. But there is a God in heaven who reveals secrets, and He has made known to King Nebuchadnezzar what will be in the latter days. Your dream, and the visions of your head upon your bed, were these..."

And Daniel 2.46-49 says,

"Then King Nebuchadnezzar fell on his face, prostrate before Daniel, and commanded that they should present an offering and incense to him. The king answered Daniel, and said, 'Truly your God is the God of gods, the Lord of kings, and a revealer of secrets, since you could reveal this secret.' Then the king promoted Daniel and gave him many great gifts; and he made him ruler over the whole province of Babylon and chief administrator over all the wise men of Babylon. Also Daniel petitioned the king, and he set Shadrach, Meshach, and Abed-Nego over the affairs of the province of Babylon; but Daniel sat in the gate of the king."

The interpretation given by God to Daniel concerning King Nebuchadnezzar's dream opened the door for Daniel to be in the King's government and led to the exaltation of the God of heaven and earth whom Daniel served. Daniel, when explaining the dream of the King, gave without hesitation honor and glory to the God of heaven who revealed it to him. He could have easily prostituted his gift by asking the King a reward in return for his service, but the Scriptures gave no mention of such. What a stark contrast to some of our contemporary ministers who are so alert to perceive how to financially capitalize from the ministry brought forth by the gifts given by God.

You see, it is the blessing of the Lord that makes one rich, and he adds no sorrow to it. Daniel gave all the glory to God. The Lord took note and touched the heart of the pagan King to raise Daniel in dignity. Verse 46 tells us that the king was so amazed by the accuracy and clarity of the interpretation of the dreams that he fell on his face and bowed in front of Daniel. I want to remind you that Daniel was a young Jewish slave taken into captivity to Babylon, brought and forced to serve the Babylonian king. God found the way to elevate His name and his son Daniel in a land that was completely foreign to him. Thus he received the command of the whole province of Babylon by the hands of King Nebuchadnezzar. A young Jewish slave was promoted to a position of prominence and authority in a country in which he was not even a citizen. After logging into the dominant position in the kingdom of King Nebuchadnezzar, it is a blessing to see that Daniel did not forget his Jewish friends who were instrumental in obtaining the answer given by the Lord concerning the dreams of King Nebuchadnezzar. In his ascension to the position of prime minister of the king, he asked the king to give the stewardship of the province of Babylon to his friends Schadrac, Meschac and Abed-Nego. In this season of apostolic invasion, the Lord wants to raise some Daniels in positions of prominence and authority to advance His kingdom on earth.

10

Joseph the Governor Prophet

GENESIS 39.1-2
"Now Joseph had been taken down to Egypt. And Potiphar, an officer of Pharaoh, captain of the guard, an Egyptian, bought him from the Ishmaelites who had taken him down there. The LORD was with Joseph, and he was a successful man..."

GENESIS 41.1
"Then it came to pass, at the end of two full years, that Pharaoh had a dream..."

GENESIS 41.14-15
"Then Pharaoh sent and called Joseph, and they brought him quickly out of the dungeon; and he shaved, changed his clothing, and came to Pharaoh. And Pharaoh said to Joseph. 'I had a dream, and there is no one who can interpret it. But I have heard it said of you that you can understand a dream, to interpret it.'"

GENESIS 41.39-44
"Then Pharaoh said to Joseph, 'Inasmuch as God has shown you all this, there is no one as discerning and wise as you. You shall be over my house, and all my people shall be ruled according to your word; only in regard to the throne will I be greater than you.' And Pharaoh said to Joseph, 'See, I have set you over all the land of Egypt.' Then

Pharaoh took his signet ring off his hand and put it on Joseph's hand; and he clothed him in garments of fine linen and put a gold chain around his neck. And he had him ride in the second chariot which he had; and they cried out before him, 'Bow the knee!' So he set him over all the land of Egypt."

GENESIS 47.5-6

"Then Pharaoh spoke to Joseph, saying, 'Your father and your brothers have come to you. The land of Egypt is before you. Have your father and brothers dwell in the best of the land: let them dwell in the land of Goshen. And if you know any competent men among them, then make them chief herdsmen over my livestock."

Joseph is a Bible character who God raised up in prominence and in governmental authority to allow kingdom advancement. Notice that Joseph did not choose himself, but rather God chose him for His divine plan. The Bible explains that although Joseph was sold as a slave in Egypt, the Lord was with him and he was a successful man; he prospered. Even though he was innocent in the accusation brought on him by the wife of his master Potiphar, Joseph was put in jail. He stayed there for a while until the Pharaoh of Egypt had a dream that he could not find answer to. Once more, we see how the Lord made a way to divinely elevate Joseph for the purpose of kingdom advancement. After the explanation of Pharaoh's dream, Joseph was raised in dignity. It was the manifestation of the power of the Holy Spirit in a secular situation for the rise of Joseph. God wants to use his Spirit that is in us to expose us in different sectors of the community, for recognition of His name and the advancement of His kingdom. By his prophetic anointing, Joseph was placed in a strategic position to ensure continuity and safeguarding of the people of Israel in a difficult period. Being governor of Egypt, Joseph was able to bless his family with a good piece of the land of Egypt.

It is undeniable that strategic positioning in the political arena confers privileges. There are doors necessary for the propagation of the Gospel, which will undoubtedly open more easily with Christians set in positions of authority in the political and governmental arenas. Then, bearing in mind that politicians have decision-making authority over the laws that govern a country; and two, that laws in a country directly affect the social, educational and economic status of residents: How then, can we significantly affect our country with the Gospel of the kingdom without infiltrating and influencing its political arena? Queen Esther, in the Book of Esther, by her strategic position in government was used to save the Jewish nation from genocide.

The time of the Church neglecting the domain of politics has passed. The Lord has released apostolic and prophetic authority in this season to uproot and kill erroneous and heretical teachings, which decimated the development of the Body of Christ and the development of the kingdom of God on earth. How many Christians have refused to enter law or political science in University for fear of being rejected by God because these curricula were supposedly not politically correct for Christians? So the devil has capitalized and has possessed some politicians for a work of mass destruction. He used Adolf Hitler to kill a large number of innocent people; and how many more politicized oppressors he has been using to drive forward his plan and his kingdom on earth. But you will know the truth and the truth will make you free. The Lord still elevates ministers in the likes of Daniel, Joseph and Esther, so that the Church may have relevance not just within the walls of a building, but in its society, implementing the mandate of the Lord to make disciples of nations.

11

Infiltrating the Marketplace

The Bible says in Acts 17.16-18,

"Now while Paul waited for them at Athens, his spirit was provoked within him when he saw that the city was given over to idols. Therefore he reasoned in the synagogue with the Jews and with the GENTILE WORSHIPERS, and in the MARKETPLACE DAILY with those who happened to be there. THEN CERTAIN EPICUREAN and STOIC PHILOSOPHERS encountered him. And some said..."

We see in this passage Apostle Paul, in his apostolic mandate, pushed to come into contact with various people in the city of Athens. And herein the Lord has allowed me to seize another key sector in our society: the marketplace. It's a place which must be affected by the Gospel if we want to have an optimal impact in a given region. For yet it is possible to have a mass of people in a given sector and have no impact; be it natural or spiritual. This phenomenon surfaces for lack of penetration by the church in the community or region.

I think the fact that Paul shared daily in the marketplace was not a coincidence. Apostle Paul had grasped that if a region would be truly affected by the Gospel of Jesus Christ, the marketplace should be influenced by the Word of God. Just as it was important to affect businessmen in the time of Paul, this principle is still as valid and dominant in the 21st century. For it is very difficult to think it possible to spread the Gospel adequately in this generation without Finances.

Ecclesiastes 10.19 says,
"...*money answers everything*."

The Word of God tells us in this declaration in Ecclesiastes that money answers everything. You need a home, money answers everything; you need a car, money answers everything; you need to eat, money answers everything. Know that money answers everything, including the Gospel. Imagine ministering without finances. Despite the fact that you could be the most anointed minister on the face of the earth, without finances, it would be very difficult to fulfill your ministry. We can surely pray in other tongues, but it can't pay for a hall rental in our region, for a conference or for a crusade; finance is needed for that. Try as a leader to go see your suppliers to tell them: "I am a man of God" when your bills are past due. Believe me it would not be long before you are visited by a bailiff, for it takes finances for ministry. Money is a necessary instrument to answer the plan of God for mankind. You can have the greatest evangelical project, but money must answer. You can have the greatest vision, but money must answer. You can have everything you need to transform your community, but money has to answer.

It is imperative to realize that the Lord knows that provision is needed for the vision. The Bible says in Proverbs 29.18, "*A people without vision perish...*," but a vision without provision will also perish. For this reason, God says in Proverbs 13.22, "*... but the wealth of the sinner is stored up for the righteous.*"

Haggai 2.7-8 states,
*"I will shake all nations, and they shall come to the Desire of All
Nations, and I will fill this temple with glory,' says the LORD of
hosts. 'The silver is Mine, and the gold is Mine,' says the LORD of
hosts."*

The question we must ask ourselves is why does the Lord want
the Desire, the treasures of the nations to come? Why the wealth of
the wicked is stored up for the righteous? Is it simply for the righteous
to buy nice houses and nice cars? Understand that it is the desire
of God that his people be blessed. He says in Psalms 35.27, he takes
pleasure in the prosperity of his servants. But much more, the Lord
is aware of the need of provision for the vision, for money answers
all things.

Every man who God sends, he also gives them provision to fulfill
the vision. The men who God anoints with a vision, he also gives
them the blessing of provision for the vision.

GENESIS 12.10
*"Now there was a famine in the land, and Abram went down to
Egypt to dwell there, for the famine was severe in the land."*

GENESIS 13.2
"Abram was very rich in livestock, in silver, and in gold."

The Bible speaks of a man named Abraham in Genesis 12.10 who
went down to Egypt because of a famine in the land of Canaan. He
stayed there for a while and returned in Genesis 13.2, from Egypt, rich
in livestock, silver and gold. Joseph, the son of Jacob, became second-
in-command in Pharaoh's government in Egypt, Genesis 41.42-43. He
was managing all the wealth of Egypt. Pharaoh established him lord
over his house and governor of all his wealth, Psalms 105.21. Solomon
received riches and honor from God, 1 Kings 3.13. And 2 Chronicles
9.22 tells us that he surpassed all the kings on the earth in riches and

wisdom; even his drinking vessels were of gold, and all the vessels of his house of the forest of Lebanon were pure gold. Not one was silver, for this was accounted as nothing in the days of King Solomon. Silver was not acceptable for this man of God, and nowadays, some believers have a problem with gold, finding it carnal and idolatrous... what ignorance! They forget that gold was created by God for the pleasure of men. All these men of God had provision for their vision.

LUKE 8.2-3

"And a certain woman who had been healed of evil spirits and infirmities : Mary called Magdalene, out of whom had come seven demons, and Joanna the wife of Chuza, Herod's steward, and Susanna, and many others who PROVIDED FOR HIM FROM THEIR SUBSTANCE."

MATTHEW 27.57

"... there came a rich man from Arimathea, named Joseph, who himself had also become a disciple of Jesus."

The Lord Jesus himself was not exempted from the principle of the necessity of provision for the vision. In his earthly ministry, he had 12 full-grown men in full-time ministry who were used to eating big fish. You should not be so naive to think that Jesus was calling down manna from heaven every day to feed his staff. The Bible clearly supports the fact that he had financial support to carry out his vision. Jesus did not simply have itinerants and poor people who followed him and who were his disciples. We see in Matthew 27.57, that he had also wealthy men of influence in his ministry. It is not surprising that he was able to accomplish his full-time ministry with the "staff" that he had. Jesus was not simply full-time but he had more than 12 full-time ministers in his ministry. Without provision, this apostolic vision certainly would have suffered. Several would say, but what about ministers like John the Baptist who wore a garment of camel skin and a leather belt around his waist, eating locusts and wild honey. He didn't seem to be rich. That's right! When I speak of finances required for the fulfillment of God's mandate, I do not speak of unnecessary wealth but provision to fulfill the vision. Certainly John the Baptist in his own right had the provision to fulfill his vision. Not only does God give the vision, he also gives the provision for the vision!

Thus, in this generation of modern capitalism, the Lord wants to deploy apostolic business ministers in the marketplace to acquire wealth: an acquisition of wealth with a divine purpose. This is not a supernatural wealth to fill one's pockets, for savings bonds, personal investments, or to secure one's second and third generation, but to lay at the apostles' feet for the fulfillment of the vision of God; wealth, but with a purpose. The Body of Christ does not need another mercenary who seeks to enrich himself by using the Gospel to his advantage but visionaries who want the riches to enrich the Gospel. I believe there is a dimension of breakthrough which the Church, sent to the nations, will have. It will require more than the tithes and offerings of the saints. It will need apostolic ministers anointed for business. Ministers sent into the marketplace not only to make money but ministers with money with a purpose. They are sent out by God into the kingdom of darkness to heap up the finances and to bring it at the apostles' feet. These spoils are for the fulfillment of the vision of God, for the vision of God can't be fulfilled without the provision. Therefore no provision no vision; and no vision no transformation of our communities for the glory of God!

We need to know that the innovative Church which will notably affect the 21st century will not just have the five-fold ministry gifts of Ephesians 4.11. Having apostles, prophets and pastors in the presbytery of a local assembly will not be able to advance the kingdom of God on its own. How relationally shallow, when everyone in a church aspires and dreams of being a five-fold minister. In fact, in certain parts of the evangelical circle, this ignorance goes as far as only recognizing a pastor as a called one of God. Therefore, when a saint is said to be having a call on his life, this literally means he will become a pastor. As pitiful as this may seem, it is still truly the state of certain parts of the Body of Christ. I dare to ask, "Can a body have only one member?" A human body with only eyes can only be a monster. The spiritual Body of Christ also would be monstrous if it would be comprised of only one multiple member. Therefore it is made of many members with different gifts and graces. In this season, God wants to strategically awaken the Church to the need of recognizing the necessary input of marketplace ministers for kingdom advancement. Those anointed ministers of God will be used to make an invasion in every sector of the marketplace in order to bring the financial abundance necessary for the fulfillment of the plan of God.

In fact, God by divine election chose some saints, before the foundation of the world, to acquire wealth by his divine power, for his work.

ROMANS 12.8

"...he who gives, with liberality..."

Some saints are simply anointed by God to give. All of God's children are called to practice the principle of tithes and offerings and of giving, but some are blessed with a divine grace to give. They are thus called to give with liberality. In Romans 12.8, notice that the verse speaks of some specific saints and not all the saints, "He who..." They are those who are anointed to give. Now it is important to understand that we cannot give what we don't have. Therefore, if the Lord calls someone to give more abundantly and liberally than the majority, he will also grant him a supernatural anointing to acquire wealth. And one of the predominant ways is by success in business.

Deuteronomy 8.18
"And you shall remember the LORD your God, for it is He WHO GIVES YOU POWER TO GET WEALTH..."

As much as God gives gifts to the Church for the development of the saints for the work of the ministry, he also gives to the church ministers with divine power to acquire wealth. I speak of a supernatural wealth, because this wealth is not acquired by human wisdom and power only but by the power of the Holy Spirit. It is a supernatural anointing for supernatural ideas, for supernatural connections and supernatural breakthroughs. The saint with that grace of God cannot be prideful about it, because it is God who gives him power to acquire wealth. These ministers do not need to live in unbearable stress; it is God who gives power to acquire... These anointed for business do not need to force the door; it is God who gives power. Business is their sphere of influence; it's there that their anointing manifests itself at full capacity. Business is their divinely appointed domain in which they are used for provision transfer.

Ecclesiastes 2.26
"For God gives wisdom and knowledge and joy to a man who is good in His sight; BUT to the sinner He gives the WORK of GATHERING AND COLLECTING, THAT HE MAY GIVE TO HIM WHO IS GOOD BEFORE GOD..."

This verse from Ecclesiastes gives us some revelations on how provision transfer takes place in the work of God. The marketplace ministers who God wants to raise up in his apostolic Church, receive from God the supernatural wisdom of God for business projects to enter the marketplace; for God seeks for transfer agents, ministers used as bridges, to transfer the finances of the world into the kingdom of God. These agents are apostolic agents who God prepares to connect with men and women who are at his service while they are yet not saved. There are businessmen and businesswomen who are presently at work gathering and heaping up funds which God will use to advance his kingdom. We need to remember that the earth is God's and the fullness thereof. Therefore God in his sovereignty having legal ownership of the riches of the earth can in any given time, decree a change of possession of his riches to advance his kingdom. Thus as someone is at work to gather and heap up finances, the Lord wants to fill a minister with his wisdom and knowledge with a business project, and idea, a strategic position in a company for a transfer of provision for his vision. Maybe as you're reading this, conviction of the Holy Ghost is filling your spirit to become a transfer agent for the apostolic mission of the Church of Jesus Christ. For it is one thing to say, "The riches of the sinners are heaped up for the righteous", but the question is, "How?" Well, here is the answer: by the kingdom of God penetrating the business world through apostolic agents of transfer.

Praying and fasting are all good but market place apostolic ministers need to be sent out: Sent out to influence, influence to possess, possess to transfer, and transfer to transform positively the orientation of nations from the grip of the kingdom of darkness to the liberty of the kingdom of light of our Lord Jesus Christ. For no money, no capacity to influence, no capacity to influence no capacity to transform our society. It is therefore why we need finances to transform our community.

Ecclesiastes 9.16 says,
"Wisdom is better than strength, nevertheless the poor man's wisdom is despised, and his WORDS ARE NOT HEARD."

Finances are necessary to affect our communities. The Bible says in this verse that the wisdom of the poor is despised and his words are not heard.

We need to acknowledge the fact that no one wants to know what the poor thinks. The poor can have a good idea which could radically change the livelihood of his community but who would listen? Do the decision makers of this world have the time or place to listen to the poor? Know that wealth gives power to speak. When you are poor, you are not given place to speak. There are certain circles in society that are virtually impossible to enter without finance and influence. You can be very anointed and wise but without money your right to speak is very restricted. Wealth gives power to speak. Imagine a meeting to discuss issues in a particular community with a rich man owning ¾ of the real estate of the area, and a poor man, both wanting to have their ideas implemented. Whom do you think would be listened to and supported? Wealth gives power to speak.

Let me give you another example. Two individuals, one rich and the other poor, have the desire to have a television show in the most popular station of the region. From your point of view, who would have it? Understand that the Christian has the greatest and most powerful message on the earth but without any vehicle to carry this message, even though it's profound, it stays worthless and fruitless. Let us realize that the vehicles are not given but bought. It therefore takes finance to spread the Gospel. It takes finance to have air times on television. It takes finance to have air time on the radio. Wealth gives power to speak and having a good platform to speak from we will have the capacity to transform our society. For faith comes by hearing.

If what the world hears on the radio and sees on television is sexual impurity, drugs and violence, certainly these subjects will have a repercussion on the daily lives of our communities. This is why the devil wants to bind the Church in poverty. For no financial prosperity, no capacity to affect and transform one's community! The devil has stigmatized Christianity as the poor man's religion. But what's worse is the evangelical leaders who support this demonic declaration of the devil by their teachings and attitude concerning finances. They are totally terrorized about speaking on finances. In fact, for many of those leaders, poverty is a sign of piety. Having run-down cars rusted without mufflers, that need to be pushed by some of their saints to start is a sign of spirituality. How ignorant and what great deception of the devil! Know that poverty can't promote influence and the lack of influence blocks the transformation of nations. Therefore, the devil says to Christians, "Preach your Gospel and I will keep you poor and your Gospel will have but a mitigated impact. Affect the poor, give them salvation and keep them financially illiterate, and I will continue to bind the rich and wealthy in order to keep their money and influence to continue to advance my agenda of destruction."

> The Bible declares in Proverbs 10.15,
> *"The rich man's wealth is his strong city..."*

Wealth is a strong city, it has power and it gives capacity to whoever possesses it. This capacity permits teaching and inculcates morals and ideologies within nations. This capacity dictates choices, the way of living, the acceptable trend for a society. This capacity gives access to communication that is able to bring transformation. Therefore television, radio and the media are available for whomever has wealth. Wealth for the rich is his fighting horse to help him acquire whatever he wants. Consequently, the devil uses the media to transmit his message and morals by using the finances of rich men and women whom he has bound. For it takes money to pay for airtime. Financial power gives capacity to teach, therefore he who has the finances, has the authority. But the devil is a liar! He will not have the last word. God is raising up the anointed for business.

In this generation, God is raising businessmen and businesswomen who will have revelation of business to transfer the funds to the apostles of God whom have the vision for the advancement of the kingdom. This will allow the apostolic Church to have the necessary finances to breakthrough in the world of communications in order to have the platform to spread the Good News of Jesus Christ.

In this generation, the anointing and revelation will be available to bring forth the marketplace ministers. The Body of Christ will not be ignorant of the need for marketplace ministers. These saints will no longer feel rejected and left out in the church dynamic. For a long time an atmosphere of false teachings on wealth persisted in the Church. It subtly released the heresy that a believer's wealth was more of a curse tending toward the possible loss of his salvation. Poverty was equal to piety and mediocrity was equal to spirituality. What mega ignorance! But the times have changed, the apostolic and prophetic voices of God are rising up with the boldness of the Holy Ghost to come against the lies of hell and proclaim the revelational truth of Christ!

There is a certain revelational methodology which needs to take place in the Church that decides to advance the kingdom. That methodology will surely bring edification to the marketplace ministers in this strategic season designated by God. The apostolic reform concerning the revelation of financial prosperity and the marketplace ministers will be necessary to break the stronghold boxing in the Church in financial stagnation. Some ministers have the finances but do not have the vision to see kingdom advancement. They only have vision for their personal kingdom advancement not working with God but from their saying ...**for** God. Others have the vision and revelation for kingdom advancement but not the finances to unfold it. Here are therefore certain keys that I believe necessary for the innovative church in order to penetrate the marketplace.

Teaching the Principles of the Kingdom on Finances

HOSEA 4:6

"My people are destroyed for lack knowledge..."

Notice this verse tells us about the people of God and not pagans who are destroyed, not because they do not have knowledge, but because they lack it. Consequently, certain Christians can receive salvation and the supernatural peace of God, know the biblical revelation of these principles and still live in poverty and profound mediocrity; because they lack biblical revelation concerning the prosperity of God. Unfortunately, in certain sectors of the Body of Christ, there is a flagrant lack of revelational teaching on prosperity. Although this comes from different valid reasons, the principles of the kingdom on finances absolutely need to be properly taught in the church in the same fashion as any other biblical principle. We cannot expect to grasp and reap the benefit of a blessing of the kingdom if it is not taught. When we speak of teaching, it is not enough for a preacher to just frantically exhort the people to give. Many a time I had the opportunity to assist preachers who lacked revelation on giving. Yet at the same time it was unfortunate to witness them exhaustingly make appeals for the saints to give. *"You've got to give; God wants you to give."* they would shout but without any trace of either anointing or revelation whatsoever. I asked God, why this spiritual awkwardness? And the Lord made me understand that the revelation of finances was lacking, in addition to the fact that the preachers themselves were not practicing what they preached. Consequently, teaching with revelation and anointing of kingdom principles on finances is the first necessary step for apostolic invasion in the marketplace and expansion of the prosperity of the Body of Christ for kingdom advancement. In these teachings, the basic revelation of tithes and offerings needs to be taught, in addition to in-depth revelation of biblical truths concerning prosperity. And secondly, they must also include revelation on finances and training of marketplace ministers capable of being sent out to get the wealth of this world for the spreading of the Gospel.

Application of Kingdom Principles of Finances

JAMES 1:22

"But be doers of the Word, and not hearers only, deceiving yourselves."

Understand that theory is good but remains useless without practice. Application of the principles on finances needs to undoubtedly follow the information and revelation received. Hearing is good but practicing is unbeatable when it comes to the principles of God. You can know theoretically the revelation of tithes, offerings, firstfruits, sacrificial offerings and even sowing, but if you do not apply them, these truths will not bring you any concrete fruit. Many believe they can manipulate God to bless them financially by applying the principle of physical healing to financial blessing. For this reason, many saints come for a laying on of hands and a prophetic prayer that they may simply receive by faith financial breakthrough. But know that you will wait for a long long time and never see your financial breakthrough if you do not become a doer of the Word and not only a hearer of the principle of tithes, offerings, firstfruits and the other principles of prosperity. For God to be able to release financial abundance in your hands, you need to be able to release from your hands what God tells you to release by the teachings of His principles on finance. Therefore, the tightfistedness with the *not much* that you have, will surely short circuit your capacity to receive the overabundance of God. All the revelational knowledge will not be enough for an enviable financial position for the Body of Christ if it does not practice the principles and revelations of God on finances and prosperity.

Penetrate, Affect and Influence the Marketplace

Other than the saints of God who practice the principles of finance, the ministers who are mandated by God to affect the business realm need to be positioned. Those ministers knowledgeable of the principles and manifesting them by a wholesome practice need to penetrate, affect and influence the marketplace. The Body of Christ needs to train marketplace ministers to be sent out. They cannot eternally stay in the prayer and fasting meetings and participate in the regular services of the local church only. They have to go out and invade the marketplace. Notice that I clearly said, *"Penetrate, affect and influence."* For it is one thing to penetrate a domain but another to make an impact and exercise influence over it. Joseph, the rich man of Arimathea, who was also a disciple of Jesus (Matthew 27.57), had wealth and influence. As the twelve were terrorized by fear and were hiding, Joseph, after the death of the Lord, claimed from Pontus Pilate Jesus' body.

> MATTHEW 27.57-60
> *"Now when evening had come, there came a rich man from Arimathea, named Joseph, who himself had also become a disciple of Jesus. This man went to Pilate and asked for the body of Jesus. Then Pilate commanded the body to be given to him. When Joseph had taken the body, he wrapped it in a clean linen cloth, and laid it in his new tomb which he had hewn out of the rock..."*

Joseph of Arimathea, this rich disciple of the Lord Jesus had so much influence that upon his demand Pilate commanded that his desire be given. He consequently received the body of the Lord which he placed, not in a secondhand tomb, but a brand new tomb worthy of a dignitary. Who said that Jesus only had poor and wasted people around him?

As much as the rich had their place in the Lord's ministry, prosperity and riches equally still have their place in modern ministry for advancing the kingdom of God. It is good to pray for the salvation of rich men at Bill Gate's level, but I believe that God wants and will raise them from amongst the people of God. He will raise them up to become agents of influence in the business realm. They'll proclaim freely and boldly the knowledge of God which is the source of their blessing and by association and relationship proclaim the salvation of Jesus Christ to non-believer colleagues, businessmen and businesswomen.

Laying the Finances at the Apostles' Feet for Unfolding the Vision of God

ACTS 4.33-35

"And with great power the apostles gave witness to the resurrection of the Lord Jesus. And great grace was upon them all. Nor was there anyone among them who lacked; for all who were possessors of lands or houses sold them, and brought the proceeds of the things that were sold, and laid them at the apostles feet; and they distributed to each as anyone had need."

The Church at Jerusalem was so blessed with financial blessings of God that no one lacked amongst them. I would like you to notice not only the fact that blessings were made available to take care of everyone but the way in which the provision was made available. The disciples who were wealthier gave finances to the apostles who were leading the Church of Jerusalem. Those saints understood that their finances were there for a goal: advancement of the plan of God. This truth definitely needs to be mastered by the modern marketplace ministers. It is one thing to call upon the blessing of God in the area of finances but another thing when that blessing comes to humbly give what God directs to give to the spiritual authority of the house to advance the work of God. Thence comes the necessity of having marketplace ministers trained. For without adequate training, it is very easy for them to fall in the traps of pride, control and the love of money when substantial funds come.

> *"In the name of Jesus, I prophesy the unlocking of a new season of identification, training and manifestation of the sons of God, businessmen and businesswomen in the Body of Christ, recognizing and submitting themselves to the revelation of the principles of prosperity and of finance in the kingdom for the advancement of the divine plan of God the Father. Henceforth in the next 10 years a supernatural manifestation of divine transfer of provision will take place from the kingdom of darkness to the kingdom of light. These transfers will be done that all shall say without any doubt that this can only take place by divine intervention of Jehovah Jireh, the providing God of provision necessary to advance the vision."*

In the first decades of this new millennium, the face of the Church is changing. Many methods and ways of ministering will change. The message of the Gospel is an eternal message but the vehicles used and the verbalization of the message are functions of many external factors. But in all that, let us understand that the kingdom of God will not cease to grow and take territories. The message of the kingdom will invade the earth and certainly the majority will recognize Jesus Christ as Lord and Savior to the glory of God the Father.

Therefore, Church of Jesus Christ, the time is neither for discouragement nor intimidation from the image which the world presents, but the time is in possessing our possession and our territory by the power of the Holy Ghost. For since the time of John the Baptist until today, the kingdom of God suffers violence and the violent takes it by force. Let the Body of Christ educate itself, infiltrate, influence and dominate every sector of society and establish the kingdom of God on the earth, for this is the innovative Church that will notably affect the 21st century.